WORDS

FROM

WITHIN

By: Taty...P

WORDS FROM WITHIN

WRITTEN BY TATYANA R. PARKS

PRINTED BY CREATESPACE

To my mother: Elaine R. Marshall

Thank you, for bringing me into this world and making me into the young lady I am today. You mean the world to me. Without you these words wouldn't flow the same. You're an extraordinary woman and I'm blessed to be your daughter.

I Love you

To my father: Broderick S. Parks Sr.

Thank you, for encouraging me. You've made incredible strides throughout the years, and you've exceeded my expectations. I know you're proud of me however, I'm extremely proud of you.

I Love You.

To my family and friends

Thank you, for just being you. Each one of you are brilliant in your own way. We may talk every day or for some every blue moon. However, I'm forever appreciative of the support you give me.

I Love you.

To the reader

Thank you, for purchasing. I hope you're inspired and you love it just as much as I do.

WORDS
FROM
WITHIN

By: Taty...P

Future Love

When the time is right and you
become mine.

We'll blend into each other's energy.

Exploring the in-betweens,

of two perfect lines of symmetry.

Afraid of Commitment

Don't shy away, because you fear

that it may be everything

you want and need.

Black on Black Crime

There is nothing sweet,

about a buffet of black bodies.

Police Brutality

The police fear for their lively hood
without reason.

In many cases,

the top of the food chain

was never endangered.

When I Look at You

Sunflowers always bloom from your
eyes.

As the healing power flows from your
voice.

Then the world stops.

When the corners of your mouth form
a smile.

Fear

There is nothing in this world to fear,

as long as God is still alive.

Hurt

I've been burned by the very people

Who claimed they loved me.

I've seen dishonesty and disloyalty up
close and personal, but

If it's just me the hurt isn't universal.

Blind in Love

Don't allow the love you carry inside to blind you.

Constantly asking the most high to deliver you, but

The signs are already here to guide you.

Embrace Yourself

Who you are,

what you possess, and

how you carry yourself

will not impress everyone.

The Lies He Tells

You believe him as he grins.

You watch the lies drip from his lips.

Yet you continue to stay.

Never Settle

Generate the life you deserve,

and never settle

for a love that is

less than your worth.

Your Inner Truth

The truth does not present itself immediately.

It's hard to trust another,

when the only person you can confide in is you.

Read the Signs

You say you love him and he laughs.

All the characteristics of your soulmate
he lacks.

I think it's time that you pack your
bags.

Never stay in a relationship you know
isn't going to last.

Breaking Point

Slowly, but soon

you'll let him go.

Slowly, but soon

Your self- esteem will grow.

Slowly, but soon

you'll close that door,

and leave him alone.

A Good Thing

One day you'll think of her.

One night you'll dream of her,

but she'll be in his arms

the man intelligent enough to know,

that you never let a good thing go.

The Difference

A girl may have hurt you,

but a woman

will rebuild you.

Tomorrow Isn't Promised

Cherish each day, because
you're on time borrowed.

Last Name

When a man loves you,

the only thing

he should want to change

is your last name.

Choose Wisely

If your partner isn't your best friend,

you're lying next to the wrong person.

The Cycle

You enable his behavior every time you take him back.

He will never love you.

Know your worth.

Hold On

Things will get better, sometimes

God puts you through the bad

to protect you from the worst.

Simple Things

Text her first,

call her,

make time for her,

show her that you care,

it's the simple things.

What He Sees

You were easy.

Now no matter what you do or say,

he will only see you as the girl

that satisfies only one need.

When You Came

I wasn't one to feel emotions,

until you came along.

.

Gold

A woman with a heart of gold,

is a very rare piece to find.

When you find her never let her go.

Secret Love

Her mind screams,

I Love You!

Too afraid to let it out,

because those three words

might cause you to walk out.

Midnight

It's 12:00 AM,

wipe your eyes, and

clear your mind.

He's not worth it tonight.

Last

I gave you my last,

and nothing

was received in return.

Sleeping Beauty

As I stare upon your face.

I pray to the lord your soul to keep,

So I may have a chance to love you
another day.

Game

I fell for your tricks,

your lies and shit.

You almost ruined me, but

this queen doesn't break easily.

Kings and Queens

You're a beautiful creature.

Your hair is one of a kind.

Your lips are rich.

Your physique is pristine.

Your skin represents 245 years of strength.

BE BLACK AND STAY PROUD

Precious Jewel

Your cookie is a special treat,

not a freebie.

Save it for the man who truly loves
you.

The man who will look you in your eyes
and say

"I do".

I can do all things through Christ who
strengthens me

Philippians 4:13

WORDS FROM WITHIN

WITHIN

A poetry book

By

Tatyana R. Parks

Instagram: @__tatyp

Twitter: @_justtaty

www.ingramcontent.com/pod-product-compliance
Lightning Source LLC
Chambersburg PA
CBHW020956030426
42339CB00005B/129